Tails of Devotion

A Look at the Bond Between People and Their Pets

Emily Scott Pottruck
Foreword by Amy Tan

Published by
tailsofdevotion.com

Tails of Devotion
3450 Sacramento Street, #350
San Francisco, CA 94118

FIRST EDITION

Printed in China by Palace Press International

Designer: Leslie Waltzer, Crowfoot Design

To Andy and Boomer
My forever pups-of-love

Perfect Companions

About eleven years ago, I attained human perfection. At one time, I thought this state of being would require years of meditation, psychotherapy, or posthumous appreciation from others. But all it took was a little dog.

Actually, there was a little preparation before the big change came about, namely, three other dogs, all of them bigger than the little dog, plus three cats (also bigger than the little dog), two rats (about the same size as the little dog), and an assortment of other playmates: one chick, a rescued baby bird, two turtles, two goldfish, a guppy and her evanescent fry, a tarantula and an iguana, a chameleon and a lizard, a salamander and a garden snake, a bull snake, a boa, several caterpillars who did not sprout wings, a tadpole who did not grow legs, and twenty-three ants who worked hard on my farm.

Most of those creatures were friends during my childhood. Although decades have passed, I remember them all, some with guilt, particularly those with sweet reptilian faces. I played with them too much, not giving them a moment's peace. Later, I forgot about them completely, leaving them to the caprices of my little brother. On at least one occasion, his curiosity proved treacherous, making it necessary later to hold a memorial service with an open shoebox, followed by burial at sea performed by pressing the toilet handle.

With my earlier companions, I chose special habitats for them. The dime-store turtles had dimestore beach-front property, a molded container with coarse sand, tap water, and a plastic coconut tree. The snakes, reptiles, tarantula, fish, and ants had houses made of glass or clear plastic, so that I, their personal voyeur, could see if they moved, and they, with one eye rotated up, could see if I, too, might do the same. Every now and then I retrieved my pals from their homes for the equivalent of a species-appropriate cuddle. The chameleon posed on my palm as I admired him with the aid of a magnifying glass. The bull snake looped around my ankles and then embraced a nearby table leg, lassoing us together. The tarantula lifted his legs high like a concert pianist's fingers, then tapped a tango up the slope of my arm.

The food I obtained for my tarantula nearly cost me my life. His preferred plat du jour was a live cricket. I procured two dozen from a vivarium and the shiny bunch was dumped into a small paper bag that was stapled shut. As I drove home, believing my tarantula's future breakfast, lunch, and dinner were well contained, the crickets must have been chowing down on the paper sack, for all at once, bugs were springing throughout the confines of my car. Crickets landed on my face and the top of my head. They slid down the back and front of my blouse. I screamed and stupidly swerved the car on the freeway, as if I could shake the crickets loose at seventy miles an hour. When I finally pulled the car to the side of the road, I flew out the door and bucked like a wild horse trying to rid myself of these insect cowboys. By the time I returned home, I had two crickets left to feed to my tarantula and had learned a valuable lesson. It is noble to do anything for a friend; just choose friends who do not require live food.

My little animal playmates taught me other lessons as well: the fragility of life, the sanctity of a good one, and the sorrow that can come in the sword slice of a second. Grief is remembering how you once filled his bowl and seeing the perpetually empty one.

The first great grief I knew for any living being was for a tabby cat I lost at age twelve. One day, she mewed by the back door as usual to be let in, but when I opened it, she dragged the lower half of her body, which must have been torn apart by a car. She purred the entire way to the vet, where she was put to sleep. Once home, I entered her name into a section of the Bible called, "Deaths," using a pencil so that I might soon erase this sad fact if I found, as I desperately hoped, that she was still mewing by the back door.

Many years later, I had another cat, a Siamese mix, whom I saw on the rainy night she was born, one of a litter of four feral kittens. She never lost her wild streak. Across her veterinary chart was scrawled in one-inch block letters: "DANGEROUS". It took three technicians in elbow-length cowhide gloves to wrangle her as she was given her rabies booster. Her Exorcist movie-strength howls,

screeches, and spitting snarls left the dogs in the waiting room quivering with ears laid low. She was a basso profundo yowler of warnings and laments. She yowled to be fed. She yowled when I returned from long book tours, refusing to eat the special treats I offered until she had thoroughly scolded me while rubbing herself against my legs, branding me once again as her own, as signaled by a purring vibrato embellished with creaky lip-smacking chirps. Those were the vocalizations relegated for the highest pleasures: eating cantaloupe rinds, stalking flies, and lounging in the greenhouse window overlooking the scrubby backyard. At age seventeen, she was found to have cancer, inflammatory bowel disease, and renal failure. Yet month after month she served as my lesson that fighters go on fighting no matter what odds are against them. She yowled and chirped for another four years.

With all these creatures, my heart widened and I found companionship for the solitary part of me that allowed no human to enter. With them, I had few flaws—nothing to be ashamed of—just the occasional shortcoming of forgetfulness of precise meal times. But I did not attain human perfection until I saw a tiny dog in a pen. That midge instantly absconded my imperfect heart.

When the tiny dog looked at me with his moist dark eyes, I saw that I had to do much better by him than all the creatures from my past. As I lifted him out of his pen, he greeted me ecstatically, as if he had known me in another life and we were at last reunited. He needed no special place to sleep other than the curve of my neck, the crook of my arm, and the bend of my knees as we lay in bed.

The tiny dog and I liked to joke that he made my husband sleep at the foot of the bed. In the morning, he jumped on my chest like a happy cricket. We played cat and mouse and took turns pouncing after one another. Whenever he saw me put on my coat or pick up my keys, he flew into his travel bag and hunkered down. If I did not pick up the bag right away, he poked his head out like a turtle and reminded me not to leave without him. If I was reading a good book, he would wiggle over and lie atop the pages so that he might absorb the wisdom of words via belly osmosis.

on the throne. At night, in bed, I listened to him sigh as he settled his body between my husband's and mine.

I would have remained perfect in this little boy's eyes had I not brought home a saucy little vixen two years later. She was even tinier than he was and a greedy pig for love. She took over the curve of my neck, the crook of my arm. For one week, the little boy dog would not look at me, and I could feel his breaking heart, because he was breaking mine. How unwavering his devotion to me had been. And I had become an untrustworthy human who had replaced him with a canine femme fatale.

And then came more lessons. I taught him to speak. I taught him to whisper. I taught him to relax, lie down, and go to sleep. Come. Sit. Stay. Look adorable. He taught me the same things. He also taught me to be patient when I was sick, to be calm when I was lost. He taught me about the power of impervious belief. He would stay by the door where he last saw me go out. By remaining at the door for hours, he made me return. He, the size of my shoe, followed me everywhere, not wanting to miss out on every fascinating thing I did. Into the bathroom he would go, watching my daily routines, my rightful place

But dogs are remarkable in their capacity to forgive—or is it that they forget and adapt? And so a week passed, and I was restored to perfection. It did not require much more than his pushing the little girl out of the crook of my arm. Fortunately, I have two arms.

Now I have two little dogs, and we three are perfect companions. As my other animal friends taught me, there is perfection in the constancy of friendship, in the absolute belief that if any of us go away, we will return. When I whisper, "Stay," my companions stay. I stay, too.

- Amy Tan

Ode to Our Perfect Companions
by Amy Tan

O perfect humans!

They let us nap in the best of spots,
A rug by their tub, the width of their bed,
the cool of their shadow by a bench in the park,
the hill of their belly, or the crown of their head.

There's the warm place they made us
when they rose from their chair.
We'll give them as thanks
a layer of our hair.

Anywhere's fine, really anywhere at all,
since that's where they are and that's what we're for,
To lend them our presence so they're never alone
When they work or they weep, as they dream and they snore.

O perfect pets!

They think that we're kissable when we yawn and first wake.
When we're sick with the flu, when our happiness is at stake.
When we win the big prize, when we go into debt.
When we fall in madly in love, when our spurned cheeks are wet.

To them we are pleasure, the meaning of life
To us they're unwavering in moments of strife.
To them we are gods for even crumbs we let fall.
To us they bring offerings of chewed shoes and old balls.

They should be immortal so that anything we face
Can be taken with thanks, humility or grace.
But if one day they're gone, then let us embrace
the day we'll rejoin for eternal fetch and chase.

Introduction

As an avid pet lover, I set out on a journey to meet other animal devotees to prove to my husband that I am not as uniquely crazy as he thinks I am. Of course, I found many: We are a very large club. As you will discover, the photographs and notes within this book tell the tales of some of the relationships between pets and their companions. Let me begin with ours.

In February 2000, Andy, my firstborn, a five-and-a-half-pound Yorkshire Terrier, was attacked by a 100 pound Husky. At first, the doctors thought his neck and back were broken. They wanted to put him down, but they soon realized that they would have to put me down at the same time.

A piece of Andy's backbone had been gnawed off by the other dog's teeth and was compressing his spine. The neurologist at the veterinary school at the University of California, Davis, did not know the severity of the ensuing paralysis and whether Andy would live or regain any use of his back muscles and hind legs.

During this traumatic ordeal, my friend Amy posted a notice of Andy's accident on a Yorkie chatboard. Within minutes I received e-mails from Yorkie owners from as far as Israel and France--virtual strangers in a virtual community. For weeks, the messages came and provided Andy and me much needed good wishes, giving me a warm sense of belonging to a group who understood our pain. I would read the missives aloud to Andy, as he lay on my chest, unable to move.

During this time, a package arrived in the mail from someone in Georgia – I did not recognize the name or the address. Inside was a pink blanket with handsewn, frilly edging. Included was a note to Andy from a woman and her Yorkie, wishing him a healthy recovery. It went on to say that this blanket was made especially for him and that it would provide comfort and love. I remember thinking at the time that she and I might be ideologically opposed on politics, or the economy, religion, or a host of other issues; yet, because of our love for our Yorkies, there was a bond between us that those without pets could not understand.

Andy's recovery was miraculous, although not complete. He has partial use of his hind legs and walks with a noticeable limp (wearing the ever-fashionable homemade baby-sock-with-duct-tape-held-on-by-a-scrunchy "cast"). He cannot jump up on the sofa or bed to sit next to whomever is there. He has leg spasms, an unstable back, and lacks control of his elimination processes. Who knew that I would be so nonchalant about cleaning up the daily messes?! It does not matter because Andy is alive. He is still our constant cuddler and big flirt, and will waddle over to my side wherever I am. And the pink blanket from our Georgia friend? That remains in his bed, one of his favorites for curling up.

My youngest Yorkie, Boomer, was with us when Andy was attacked. Though he trembled with fear and was covered in Andy's blood, he was unharmed—physically; but he was traumatized psychologically and is to this day. Boomer is now afraid of other animals and often hides behind me. Thinking that I am his first line of defense, he "velcroes" his body to mine in the morning and at bedtime. I have become his personal security blanket.

Yet he is our loyal guard dog and works the 8 a.m. to 4 p.m. shift. From inside the safety of our home, Boomer barks at every dog who walks by. Off duty, Boomer prefers to be up on any pillow so he can monitor any activity, or he will hide in the darkest of places—I think to rest up for sentry watch.

Over the past six years, my bond with these two Yorkies has grown stronger than I ever thought possible. This has led me to stop and pet every dog that walks across my path (except for Huskies). I started collecting dog books. Name the pet store and I have "been there, bought that." I also became a vegetarian. I can no longer imagine eating anything that has a face.

I've also noticed that wherever I go, I end up meeting and talking to the other animal lovers in the room. This connection to Andy and Boomer opened my life to a whole new group of people, and we are thrilled to be able to talk to someone about our furry children.

Thus the inspiration for this book: the devotion between people and the animals that we live with, care for, and are cared by. I do believe that a more accurate title for the book would be *Tails of Devotion, A Look at the Bond Among People and Their Pets and Other People*. We all recognize the bond that we extend to other animal lovers. I believe it transcends many differences among us.

The 58 subjects in this book confirm that belief. During the photo sessions, I watched each person's face relax and smile as he or she talked about the animals in their family. Lindsay described Blue, her lizard, in the same glowing terms as Walter used for Happy, his black Labrador.

Marsha described the different moods and idiosyncrasies of Oscar, her "grand rabbit," with the same degree of parental knowledge as Connie had about Mr. Peeps, her cat.

There are those brave and caring souls who rescue sick, injured, neglected, or abandoned pets who are destined for an early death. Melinda saved her blind cat, Wilbur, who follows her voice and has learned to navigate his surroundings. Sherri, whom I call the original dog whisperer, not only has rescued and adopted six dogs for herself to mother, but she has also trained the most unsociable of dogs so they can be placed in loving environments elsewhere. Kay and Yoshigo have built a haven for stray cats that covers their entire yard. What a sight to behold: a woman in her seventies, squatting as she dips under the protective netting in the yard to give each cat a treat or a hug.

No matter how long our animals have been with us, our mutual devotion is unflagging. Nancy's dog, Sage, has been with her for 16 years—prior to the days of marriage and motherhood. Seven-year-old Arryssa has had Eve, her snake, for three years and talks about their "growing up" together. Mimi, age 88, views her Siamese cat, Banjo, as her best friend, albeit with many quirks. Like we all do with friends, she recognizes that the positive attributes far outweigh the negative ones. I think about these families often. They welcomed me

into their homes, let me play with their animals, and shared their personal stories with me. I am forever changed from meeting Elizabeth and her German Shepherd, Hero. Elizabeth is homeless and, when I met her, lived in an abandoned trailer in a junkyard at the edge of San Francisco. The night before I met her, she broke up a dog fight and was badly bitten. She had a hole in her leg large enough for my fist to go into and had spent the morning at San Francisco General Hospital's emergency room.

On the cold, rainy day when Lacy Atkins and I arrived to take their photograph, Elizabeth led Hero to the spot we had chosen and took off his muzzle. When Lacy and I took one step forward, Hero ferociously barked to warn us to stay away. Frankly, we were very wary as Elizabeth held on to this 90 pounds of solid muscle just by his collar. The images Lacy captured do not show his fierceness and protectiveness. They do show the connection between these two souls who feel disconnected from most of the rest of the world. In that moment, Elizabeth and Hero were identical to everyone in the book—the surroundings and the living conditions were of no consequence.

Unfortunately, the more I ventured into the relationship between people and animals, the more I learned about the cruelty some humans inflict on these innocent creatures. We've all heard or read the sickening, heart-breaking stories. Yet no matter what you might read in the newspapers or see on TV, nothing can prepare you for meeting these animals in person—the pain, the physical punishment, the total lack of care, the fear that man has instilled in these animals is a living nightmare.

It is amazing to see the resiliency of these animals and their willingness to trust and feel devoted to another person again. The staff and volunteers of the shelters and animal welfare organizations are the angels who walk among us. They are the rescuers, the caregivers, the trainers. Their patience and constant work have rehabilitated the most damaged of animals. You need only to look at the before and after photos to see that the new lives given to these animals truly are miraculous. The services they provide help pet guardians become better parents. They offer assistance to those people who do not have the economic capacity to cover all veterinary costs. I will be forever in awe. And I have learned that there is always hope in what appears to be the most hopeless of circumstances.

That is why all the proceeds from the sales of *Tails of Devotion* are going to five San Francisco organizations that create the miracles: the Friends of San Francisco Animal Care and Control, PAWS (Pets are Wonderful Support), Pets Unlimited, Rocket Dog Rescue, and The San Francisco SPCA. In the middle of this book is further information on the work of these nonprofit organizations and how to contact them. Please consider sending them an additional donation. They need our financial support to continue their selfless acts of kindness.

Many of the animals that appear in the following portraits were rescued by families who wanted to provide love, food, shelter and all the other ingredients for a new life. An "*" next to the animal's name indicates this special trait.

To be as inclusive as possible of all pet lovers, pages 126-127 are for you to insert your photos and letter. Welcome to our world!

Like all good tales, this has been an emotional journey with many happy endings. I hope the stories also resonate with you. May they make you smile, cry with joy, laugh, and, of course, cause your tail to wag.

Warmly,

— Emily

Dear Fanny,

We love you so much. We have one question though. Why do you always bark at the door even if it is one of us?

You are the best dog.

Love,
Rosie, Sophie, Zeke, Abie, Ayelet, and Michael

Sophie Chabon

Ayelet Waldman, Michael Chabon, Rosie, Sophie, Zeke, Abie
Fanny, Burmese Mountain Dog

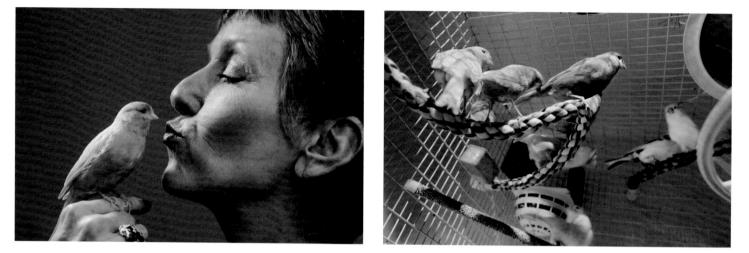

Who would have thought that a pair of Canaries would have created a situation where we would build an entire room just for you and the many others that have followed. Like so many other humans, we originally got you because you were cute, and we loved the idea of your pretty singing in the mornings. It didn't occur to us that you would all have such distinct personalities and attitudes.

Just like your feline brother and sister, you impact us daily. Watching you play, take naps, establish hierarchy and build your nests has been a treasure. Occasionally you get a little demanding about your daily fresh organic fruits and greens - and fuss because we forgot the bits of apple.

Seeing the world through your bright little eyes has been a lesson and a joy — and sometimes a heartache. We're better humans with you in our lives.

PJ and Dan Jamin

David and PJ Jamison
Miss Peep, Red Factor Canary; Yani*, Domestic Short Haired Calico

CITY OF OAKLAND

Official Memo

JERRY BROWN
Mayor

To: Mayor Jerry Brown

From: Dharma Brown
First Dog of Oakland ("FIDO")

Date: August 17. 2005

As you know, I take my responsibilities as First Dog of Oakland ("FIDO") very seriously. These duties include a daily security check of City Hall. I have carried out my sniffing duties with zest and diligence. The following is a summary of my findings for the last month:

(1) <u>Unwanted visitors</u>: none
(2) <u>Unlawful substances</u>: none
(3) <u>Other security risks</u>: none
(4) <u>Negligently stored food items</u>: 5 sandwiches and other lunch bag items in open desk drawers, 1 "goodie" basket left on someone's desk, 17 wastebaskets with left-over food tidbits, 14 candy bars and other sweets in various locations, 3 soft drinks spilled on floor, 8 other unidentifiable (in human terms) food-like substances (but they sure tasted good to me). I promptly handled the "clean up" operation for all of the above items.

On another note, I understand there have complaints about my snoring and barking during meetings. While I feel there is some justification for my actions (those meetings are boring and wouldn't we have more fun playing "fetch"?), I will try to curb this behavior in the future.

Your faithful canine companion and loyal servant to Oakland,

Dharma

Cc: Anne Gust Brown, First Lady of Oakland

Mayor Jerry Brown and Anne Gust Brown
Dharma, Black Labrador

Simple Pleasures
I forget the simple pleasures.
Joey, you remind me everyday.
Time with family
a long walk on the beach
some food
and a nap.
Life is good.
Thank You.

Cassidy Moore and David Carradine, Sotia
Joey*, Pit Bull

5-10-05

Kitty: Meow, Meow, Someone dumpped me in here in your garage. I'm very hungry. plspls. feed me. Meow, Meow. I have not been eaten any food for a few days. Meow. Meow.

KAY: Who is crying in my basement. Oh oh Kitty, Kitty. What are you doing? you are crying!

Kitty: Meow, meow, feed me sooon, feed me. I am starving, I am starving to death.

KAY: Wait here Kitty. I'll bring food right way.

Kitty: Meow, Meow, Mama, Mama, where is my mama. I'm hungry. hungry.

KAY: Kitty, Kitty, food is here, eat, eat and eat.

Kitty: Oh, food is so good, meow, meow. I can not stop eating food.

KAY: You are so beautiful. Kitty. I'll keep you here and you will never be hungry again. Kitty. Kitty.

Kitty: Thank you, Thank you, I want to give you kiss. Meow. Meow.

KAY: Are you sure, you have not been eaten any mouse.

Kitty: Thank you, Thank you, mama mama. now I am 4 years. I'm very happy in here, big yard to play, a lot of food and a lot of cats. meow, meow.   KAY.

Mikey

Kay and Yoshitsugu Yoshii
Miki*, Cat

DreamBoy

Azul

Elissa (MOM)

Tiger

Nipper

Paul

Elissa: This is so great! Everyone I love. Wish the cats and chickens could be here too . . .

Nipper, Paul, Tiger: Why do we have to stand so close to him? Can't we just run around? We have to pee and so much calling for us to smell - so much to do and so little time . . .

Dreamboy: I can do this, stand here, but I'd prefer to eat and stand. Who are these women and why don't they have carrots for me - I like to be paid for this, don't they realize horses have a Union? Didn't my mom make that clear beforehand? Oh well, I am a dignified Quarter Horse . . .

Azul (14 yrs): Sure I love Animals, but I'd rather be with my friends. I'm hungry. When can I go? . . . .

Elissa Eckman, Azul
Dreamboy*, Horse; Nipper*, Paul*, Tiger*, Greyhounds

Sreed Haran
Tabby*, Tabby Cat

SREED :- HOW ARE YOU DARLING, HOW WAS YOUR DAY - WELL I AM
GLAD TO SEE YOU CAME HOME TO WELCOME ME

TABBY :- IT WAS NICE DAY - THE SUN WAS OUT AND I WAS SUN
BATHING. ON ANOTHER NOTE DID YOU BUY MY TREATS

SREED :- SORRY I COULD NOT GO TO THE SUPERMARKET, BUT I
WAS CLOSE TO TRADER JOE'S AND I FOUND SOME
TREATS THERE SO I BOUGHT THEM.

TABBY :- LET ME SEE!   LET ME SEE!
OPEN THE JAR AND PUT SOME OUT FOR ME TO
TASTE
YUK YUK YUK - I DO NOT LIKE THIS - THIS
IS CHEAP - WHERE IS MY EXPENSIVE TREATS?

SREED :- SORRY MY DEAR, I DID NOT HAVE THE TIME
TODAY TO GO TO THE SUPERMARKET

TABBY :- WELL I EXPECT TO HAVE MY REGULAR TREATS
TOMORROW. DO NOT FORGET, OTHERWISE YOU
WOULD BE ABLE TO PAT ME AS I WOULD BE
VERY MAD

SREED :- SORRY, SORRY, I PROMISE TO GET
THIS BY TOMMORROW

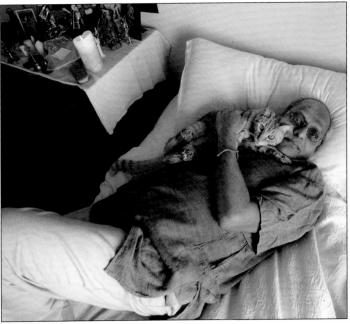

To My Family,

I love you very much, but we need to discuss this travel thing. PLEASE STOP There... we've discussed it

Love,
KIWI

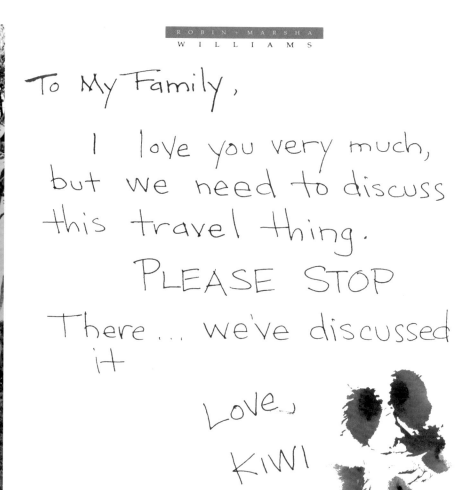

Robin and Marsha Williams, Cody, Zelda
Kiwi and Mizu, Standard Poodles

Oskie
     Who would have ever thought - A RABBIT!!
It is strange - would certainly not have
been our first choice. It was all Beth - we don't
know where she got the idea of you - went
to a fish store in Downtown Oakland with
Josie and there you were. You looked like
a white rat but you were home by the
time we saw you - you had a name, a cage
(never used), a room (actually 2) and Beth
already loved you. Michy too. I asked if
you shed (Oh no!! they don't shed the
sisters said) We believed you - Ha!!
Figured you were too small to ruin
anything - Ha again!!
     All that said Oscar Rabkin, we
love you in a way we really never
thought possible. We get you. Although
to most you don't seem to communicate,
we have learned to read your ears +
body movements... You are our zen
bunny. You are content, happy, angry,
anxious. You lick, you cuddle.
You are a sun worshipper like the
rest of us, you love organic greens
and you love us!!
     Love Grandma and Grandpa.

Marsha and Larry Rabkin
Oscar, Bunnie

Barbara

Bunkers I've always wanted to tell you how special you are. You make me 😊 even when I'm sad. Rambo your an wonderful addition to our family.

Glendon

Rambo I've wanted to tell you how funny you are. How you run up and down the stairs at night. Why do your eyes look red at night but their blue in the day. Bunkers why do you wait til I'm sleep and Jump on my bed.

Emil

Bonkers you were the nicest most Gentle cat I had ever known.. you were always there when any of us needed you. Rambo you really made an impact on this family. I Know you'll really take this family on a ride, and welcome to the family.

LaShundra

Rambo you are so sweet your the most intergetic yet calm cat I know. Bonkers you Just crazy running all around giving people the eye but yet your my Sunshine.

Raytrina

Bunker no words can explain my love for you but since were talking I love you sooooooo much, Rambo where did you get your energy from share your secret so I can stay Awake in class.

Guys Your all the greatest I think I'm the luckiest cat in the WORLD to have such wonderful family members like You. Love Bunkers.

Barbara Glaspie, Glendon, Christopher, La'Shundra, Emil, Raytrina, Jouonte
Bonkers*, Rambo*, Cats

Mickey and Caryl Hart, Reya
Tyler, Doberman ; Ally, Papillon; Vikku, Vietnamese Pot Belly Pig; Sequoia, Arabian Horse

Ally, Vikku and Tyler,

Ally you are an energetic, fun pup that we love so much. Since the first time we saw you poking your head though your crate, you've brightened up our lives. We are your slaves, you spoiled little girl!

And Vikku, when we imagine your perfect life, you are sitting in a rocking chair in New Orleans sipping a mint julep, eating a giant crème pie and talking with your rich southern accent (even though we know you are a Vietnamese pot-belly pig). We love it when you make us laugh.

Tyler - when you came to our family, you were just as energetic as little Ally. We love you so much! We know you have thoughts of devouring poor Ally, and we really appreciate you holding back.

To our owners,
— Why don't you give us more food!!! We love food, especially bones for us dogs and more watermelon and berries for Vikku. You are great owners & pals, but we would appreciate it if you would... no just make with the food.
— I love it when I slow my breathing down so you think I'm dead. You guys are suckers, always rushing over to me fearing the worst & I laugh so hard when you poke me to see if I am alive. This always makes my day!! — VIKKU

FOR   ZAIDIE

There once was a roguish dog named Red,
Sporting lots o' wavy hair on his head,
He came home with Cindy,
Befriended kit-Zaidie,
And thought life would be calm in his bed.

Along came Maman, Eli and Beanie,
The Kelpie dog who at times was queenly,
Making themselves at home,
Through Bernal Hill would roam,
They settled into their lives routinely.

Suddenly rescue-dog-Roz did enter,
After a long, lonely, rainy winter,
She hid her true self,
'Neath her hunting stealth,
An antipodal angel had sent her.

"No dog zone!" for crazed Eli did beseech,
Rolling o'er the stinky stuff on the beach,
The three dogs would wrestle,
Out o'way Zaidie did hustle,
Sit, don't beg, in vain they would try to teach.

Household awry, morn' feeding does await,
Keeping their lives in o'er chaotic a state,
All tucked in the king bed,
Goodnight to all is said,
Happily e'er after, succumbed to fate.

RED

BEAN

ROZ

Love, Nini (aka Cindy), Maman (Traci) ELI

Traci Des Jardins and Cynthia Blair, Eli,
Bean*, Kelpie; Roz*, German Hunting Dog; Red, Irish Terrier

Anthony Alonzo, Aryssa
Eve, Python Snake

Aryssa:
I Love you Eve because you are my baby for almost four years, and you were so small when I got you. You are almost as long as I am, and were growing together!! together!!

Eve:
I Love you as a mom, and I wish I could be with you all the time.

Dearest Arnie,

You were rescued from the Fresno SPCA and adopted by the San Francisco Hearing Dog Program. You were given the name, Arnold, by the trainers after the California governor but we call you Arnie. Due to your excellent training success, you were placed with us. It was a perfect fit.

We fell in love with you when we saw you for the first time. You are a happy, fun-loving, and hard-working poodle. Our grandkids adore you. Ryan (7 years old) is thrilled when you cuddle in his lap. Conor (18 months old) has been terrified of dogs but not of you. He went up to you, gently petted you and said "Nice doggy." Our other grandchildren live in South Dakota and see you frequently on the web cam.

For 14 years, we had a beloved hearing dog named Scotty. He gave us independence, and tremendous love. He alerted us to a gas leak and could have saved our lives. We miss him dearly, but you have filled the gap and become an important member of our family. You will be our ears. We love you.

Jim and Nancy

Jim and Nancy Cummins, Doreen Murphy, Conor
Arnold* (Hearing Dog), Poodle

Mimi Silbert
Amnesty*, Border Collie, Australian Sheperd, Golden Retriever Mix

Dear Amnesty,

It feels odd to write you; we talk so often and openly, there's little left unsaid. You already know how much you mean to me. Your constant love, loyalty, generous, forgiving, and brave spirit keep me going. Even more, are the Delancey Street values you embody.

You hold no grudges. You take responsibility for your mistakes (always bringing me the empty containers of my cookies you've eaten). You herd us together daily to remind us how much we need each other. And despite early abuse, cancer, and numerous illnesses, you're never grumpy, self pitying or self-absorbed: you're always GIVING. Mostly, you know that HOPE WILL TRIUMPH OVER DESPAIR. Why else would you believe each day that you'll get a taste of my daily Hot Fudge Sundae, when for 7 years, I haven't shared even a drop?!

I guess there is one thing I've never told you. And it's important because it's the way you "keep me in my place" and remind me what really matters.

A while back we went to talk to a resident who had screwed up badly. I talked for several hours, explaining what he needed to do to break his repeated self destructive cycle. He listened, he cried, I felt he understood, we hugged. The next day I received a large thank you card from him. "Oh," I thought (getting a little full of myself). "He's thanking me for helping him make this breakthrough. How wonderful!"
I opened the card and found this note:

" Dear Mimi,
    For the rest of my life, I'll never forget Amnesty licking away my tears. She believed in me when I didn't believe in myself."

How silly we humans can sometimes be. What more can I say after that — Except, OK — one little taste of my hot fudge is in order . . . .

            Love, Mummy

Dear Kids:

Thank you for bringing so much joy to our lives and for constantly making each day a new adventure. You are each so special and unique.

"Murphy": You started it all. The irresistible "fluff ball" in the L.A. pet shop. We just had to have you. Now the oldest but still irresistible

"Minnie": The matriarch. Our "old lady" So easy going and loyal. You demand so little and give so much!

"Holly": The alpha dog. Our little tomboy. Shy with strangers but affectionate with friends

"Itsy": Three pounds and the heart of a lion. Our attack dog. The group enforcer

"Buckley": I know, I know ... The world around you is so big and so scary. But don't worry. We will make sure that you are safe.

T.J.: Lover boy. Any lap is paradise ... as long as dad is not too far away.

"Charlie": You live in Charlie's World. A world that has not been discovered by humans.

We are so lucky to have you in our lives.

DAD and Dad

Ed Valencia and Terry McCarthy
Murphy, Minnie, Holly, Itsy, Buckley, TJ, Charlie, Yorkshire
Terriers

Dear Cutey,
Thanks for sharing with us the joy of Hopping, the warmth of nose nuzzles, the peace that comes from just Kicking back on the cool, green grass. But most of all thanks for teaching us that caring & Compassion Starts with a carrot!

Your Human Family

CUTEY

Jessica Aguirre and Jay Huyler, Isabella, Olivia
Cutey, Dutch Rabbit

Dear Mom,

What a great, well-travelled 12 years we've had together! I remember when Bacchus & I were puppies and you brought us home to that big house in New Jersey. My favorite things about that house were the wide-open wooden floors that we used to slide on, the delicious tasting baseboards and the pool! Bacchus' favorite things were the big hill in the backyard where he'd chase me around in the snow in the winter, and your tomato garden.

Boy, was it a big change moving from there to live with Aunt Kelly & Uncle David in Texas 5 years later. Thank goodness you had the super-size custom-built air-conditioned dog house built for us! I loved it! Bacchus did too until the day that I ripped up the beds and he got freaked out by the bits of foam flying around — what a weenie! We loved Kelly and David, but we missed you soooo much, so we were ecstatic when you bought the house with the yard in San Francisco. It's never hot here, you take us out to see other dogs in that cool park in the Presidio (the one with all the cute gophers) and we have the world's nicest dog walker!

I know you misss Bacchus since he died in February. He talks to me regularly in my dreams from dog heaven. He is very happy — he can run again — and he can see that you and I have bonded even more. He tells me to take special care of you now that you're sick — which I do by sleeping at the foot of your bed and being extra sweet! I love you, Mom! Layla

Jana Thompson
Layla, Golden Retriever

Jason Kent
Rocky*, Pigeon

Rocky the Rock Dove (Pigeon)

I guess if I could communicate with Rocky, I'd ask the following:

A. Why do you throw half of your very expensive seed on the floor?

B. Why do you hide under the couch and ambush people when they walk by with bare feet?

C. Why do you take advantage of my socks that are on the floor?

D. Why can't you do your business on the newspaper instead of all over the house?

E. Do you really need to take your baths with bottled water?

His answers would be!

A. After five years you should know what seed I like

B. Because its fun

C. I don't have to share my seed with socks.

D. I like watching you clean it up.

E. Yes!

Reverend Cecil Williams and Janice Mirikitani
Yuki*, Cat

Lunch

Janice: I'm in control here.

Cecil: I'M in Control!

Yuki: Huh. that's what they think. I'M in control!

Breakfast

Janice: My cat loves me!

Cecil: My Cat loves ME!

Yuki: i love the hand that feeds Me!

Dinner

Cecil: I love this Cat. She's independent. Free! Unpredictable. Like Me!

Janice: Yuki is a female warrior. She goes after moths, spiders, shadows on the wall. She's quick, vigilant watchful. Like me!

Yuki: these humans are so weird. (Yawn) where's the food?

Simon Rhim and Sarah Felumb
Lily, Chow/Border Collie; Panda*, Border Collie/German Short Hair Pointer

Lily and Panda remind us to be silly and thoughtful, gentle and true for our most basic needs. We wake, eat, move, develop. Breathing beside one another. Dreaming beside one another.

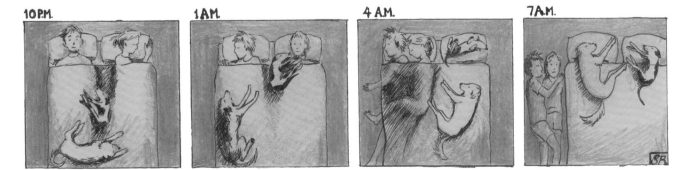

M.C

IF I COULD TALK TO M.C, I WOULD ASK HER WHY DOES SHE POOP EVERYWHERE. BECAUSE EVERYTIME I PUT HER DOWN SHE POOPS. AND WHEN I ACCIDENTLY HURT HER SHE PUTS HER BUTT IN MY FACE WHEN SHE CLIMBS UP MY ARM AND POOPS ON MY SHOULDER. BUT I WOULD ALSO LIKE TO UNDERSTAND WHAT SHE SAYS WHEN SHE SQUEAKS BECAUSE SHE DOES IT ALOT AND IT GETS ON MY NERVES BUT IT WOULD BE REALLY GREAT IF I COULD TALK TO HER AND GET TO KNOW HER MORE BECAUSE I WOULD REALLY LIKE TO KNOW WHAT IT'S LIKE FROM HER POINT OF VIEW.

Monique Sala

Frisco

When we first got Frisco, he was 4 weeks old. He was so small we could hold him in our hands. We had to mix his milk by hand, and feed him with a small baby bottle. He would wake up in the middle of the night and cry like a little baby, so we would have to get up and feed him. As Frisco got older and grew bigger, he had to get shots. Once he got those he graduated from the house, to the backyard. Friscos Grandmother made him a nice big dog house, by hand, and even put vertical blinds on it, so he don't get a draft. Now he's so big, and used to his house and backyard. He has all kinds of room to run and play. Friscos favorite thing in the world is to chew on things. What ever comes his way gets teeth marks. He's a really good dog and loves to play. He's good with everyone. We all love him and have our own special time with him. My nick name for Frisco is "Piggy", because when he gets excited he grunts like a little pig. I think if Frisco could talk or we could understand each other, he would tell me where he wants to go today for a walk.

Shanna Trujillo

Frisco

If I could talk to Frisco I would love to tell him to PLEASE STOP pulling me so fast. I would teach him things like how to call me in case of emergency and not to destroy everything in the back yard, but most of all I would tell him I love him. when we go for rides in my truck we can tell eachother jokes and listen to music together. Sometimes he just looks at us with these really sad looking eyes and I wish he could tell me whats wrong. when he's hungry he makes a noise with his food bowl it would be nice if he could say I'm hungry now. I really believe that our relationship would be alot closer than what it is if we could talk to eachother.

DeJuan Redwood

Frisco

If me and my dog were able to communicate I think that we will have a lot to talk about. For example when I take him on walks he always has to stop to sniff everything. If we talked I would tell him to keep on walking until we get to where we are going. Also I think that he would tell me when he's bored or when he's hungry, cause he don't talk and when he is hungry he pushes his bowl around and makes a lot of noise. He would also tell me about how his day was, or how much he needs a new house because he chews on it all day, but I think that we would have a better relationship than we do now.

Alex Trujillo

DeJuan and Shanna Redwood, Monique, Alex
Frisco*, Pit Bull; MJ*, Guinea Pig

Isabel Allende and William Gordon
Olivia*, Tibetan Terrier

Olivia and I don't need words to communicate. She has trained me well. She wags her tail and I obey. If she could talk and I could bark, our dialogue would be something like this:

O. – Wake up, Isabel, it's already 6:30 am.

I. – Is this negotiable? It's Sunday and it's raining! Can we wait until it's light out there?

O. – You decide. You're the human. What is a bladder ready to burst compared to my suffering before I was rescued by the Humane Society?

I. – Beat it! You sound like my mother.

O. – Your mother was rescued too? The poor woman...

I. – I mean, emotional blackmail.

O. – What? I've never blackmailed you. I am a very grateful dog. Go on sleeping while I sit by the door and wait patiently. Don't worry about me. I would rather die of an internal organ explosion than pee on your rug.

I. – Okay, okay, don't take it personally. See? I am getting up right now. Just take your paws off me and please don't French kiss me.

John Hurley and Justin Hafen, Sydney
Henry, Old English Sheepdog

Dear Henry,
     We just wanted to write you a note
to tell you how much we love you! We love
you _so_ much because you give us unconditional
love... Kiss us uncontrollably when we come home,
follow us everywhere we go, sit and stare at
us and let us use you as a big fluffy pillow!
     Who could have thought that you would
become such an important part of our family?!?
     We love you more than you'll ever know!
          All our love
          and
          more,
          Sydney, Justin & John

P.S.
If you must chew on a shoe, please, use one of
   my dads!!

Dogs will love you
no matter what!!

Mother's Day 2005

Dearest Banjo:

It has been almost 3 yrs. since you snuggled into my life and I cannot imagine any years without you being a part of them since that first morning you bit me on the ear (Left) and meowed that it was 5 A.M. and you were starving to death and did I have no sympathy for starving animals. Banjo you were Right. At 5 A.M. I have no sympathy for starving animals or creatures. But here is where love steps in. One look and I was in love with this Little bunch of gray Fluff, wiskers long enough to tickle my nose and baby blue eyes that would give Frankie a run for his money any day. It's funny, after 3 yrs I am the one who cannot sleep after 5 A.M. and can do so only after I know Banjoc has had his breakfast and is sleeping peacefully on my stomach and snoring happily in my ear (Ra) What won't we do for our kids and our cats or our cats and our kids? You tell me!

At the beginning of Banjo's 4 yr, he has doodloped another Talent. He opens the front door — not physically. He just sits in front of it, and sure enough when I see him sitting there I know some one is on the other side. He hasn't failed me yet! The same is True of his morning oatmeal. When he smells it cooking in the microwave he Jumps up on his chair — cleans his wiskers and is ready for breakfast — then we all go back to bed!

Banjo I salute you! and I love you!
your Mama Mimi
xx

Mimi Godchaux
Banjo*, Siamese

Karen and Ronnie Lott, Isaiah, Chloe, Hailey
Lucy, Australian Sheperd; Rascal, Rabbit

Lucy, you are the epitome of unconditional love. Your love and commitment to our family never ends. Your desire to protect us overrides all reason... You are the greatest guardian of our world. Lucy, you let me have fun _Always_! I can always count on you to be happy. You light up the room with your happiness and joy! Lucy, you bring me happiness on a rainy day. Your love for our family stretches out for miles, farther than the eye can see. Lucy, I can tell you all my secrets. I love that you are with us, it's so great. You are very considerate, you are great to us. Lucy, you are the best. Why? Your Love and kindness!

We love you so much Lucy

Claire
Bunni
Mommie & Chloe
Hailey

Mom and Dad, thanks for choosing me from the litter. I was very excited to join the Newman family on Washington Street.

* It was love at first sight.

Our garden is so beautiful with all the bulbs and plants you put in it. Why can't I roam around and dig there?

* Digging just doesn't help bulbs grow.

When does duck hunting season begin? You know I'm a water dog. I can't wait!

* You are a great retriever. I wish there were more ducks and I was a better shot.

Walking in the Presidio is fun. Why do I always have to stay on the leash. I wouldn't hurt anything if I ran free.

* It's the law. It's a federal offense too.

Come on, throw the ball some more. You can't tire me out.

* Yeah, but you can sure wear our arms out.

Ellen and Walter Newman
Happy, Black Labrador

Elizabeth Drury
Hero*, German Sheperd

You are my heart beat
    my Blessing daily
the essence of devotion

You keep hope alive within
    me while all about me
Rust & Crumble

Trusting Strong and True
    you are my HERO.

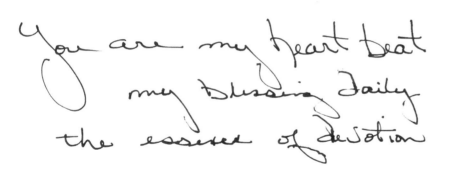

paws
Pets Are Wonderful Support

Pets are Wonderful Support

At PAWS (Pets Are Wonderful Support), we realize the best real estate in San Francisco is a place called home. It's a neighborhood where our clients and their animal companions live together without the worry of loneliness, lack of food or fear of separation because of their health or financial circumstances.

People with long-term disabilities can face many losses: health, employment, economic security and sometimes, the support of family and friends. PAWS understands that often a pet can be one's only source of comfort and that a pet's unconditional love can help ease depression and despair, especially in the case of a life-threatening illness. Since 1987, PAWS has provided comprehensive services in our Companion Animal Support Services program – a pet food and supply bank, dog walking, cat care, grooming, supplemental and emergency vet services, transportation to vet appointments, and pet foster care when clients need long-term hospitalization – all designed so our clients can maintain the love and companionship of their companion animals.

Our Education program reaches out nationally to medical and veterinary practitioners with publications on the health benefits of pets and information on how to reduce the risk of disease transmission between animals and people. Our Client Advocacy program ensures that disabled persons are aware of their rights to have service animals in public accommodations and housing.

Because of the generous support of the community, in 2005 PAWS is able to annually serve nearly 500 human clients and their 600+ pets in the Companion Animal Support Services program and reach thousands more through our Education and Client Advocacy programs. For more information about PAWS, and to read about our exciting plans for the future, please visit us online at www.pawssf.org.

PAWS, 645 Harrison Street, Suite #100
San Francisco, CA 94107
Tel: 415.979.9550, Fax: 415.979.9269
E-mail: info@pawssf.org

OUR MISSION
PAWS is a volunteer-based organization that improves the health and well-being of low-income persons disabled by HIV/AIDS and other illnesses by offering them emotional and practical support to retain the companionship of their pets, by educating the community on the benefits and risks of animal companionship, and by advocating on behalf of the human-animal bond.

OUR VISION
PAWS envisions a society that honors the vital role that companion animals have in the lives and well being of humans, where a lack of financial resources or physical abilities never threaten to separate humans from their animal companions, and where the physical, emotional and social benefits of the human-animal bond are incorporated into the health care and social service delivery systems.

HOW YOU CAN HELP
Volunteer. Join our dedicated team of over 350 active volunteers and provide direct support services like dog walking, grooming, cat care, transportation services and foster care. Or help us behind-the-scenes in the planning of our annual extravaganza, Petchitecture, or the always fabulous, Doggone Fun Run.

Donate. PAWS depends entirely on the support of individual donors and private foundations to support our annual operations. Your monetary donations or planned gift will make a direct, lasting impact in the lives of our clients and their companion animals.

Collect. Each week, PAWS distributes hundreds of pounds of pet food and supplies to help feed and support our clients' companion animals. Consider hosting a food drive and help us keep our shelves full of canned cat and dog food and, the always in need, cat litter.

The San Francisco SPCA

Since 1868, the San Francisco Society for the Prevention of Cruelty to Animals (The SF/SPCA) has set the standard for compassionate animal care in the Bay Area and around the nation. Throughout our long and distinguished history we have been in the forefront of progressive and innovative animal welfare achievements. Over the years, the Society has introduced many pioneering programs and services, and today our work has made us a leader in saving the lives of homeless dogs and cats.

The SF/SPCA's groundbreaking Maddie's Pet Adoption Center, opened in 1998, has forever altered the traditional concept of an animal shelter. With its light and airy dog and cat living quarters, the center is a place of life and hope where homeless companion animals receive training, socialization and love to better prepare them for a new life. All shelter dogs and cats are altered prior to adoption. They also receive vaccinations, microchipping and a 30-day medical assistance plan. Homeless animals receive any necessary medical treatment at

The SF/SPCA Hospital, which also offers a full range of veterinary services to the public, including low-cost medical treatment for the pets of San Francisco seniors, and other qualified individuals.

The SF/SPCA offers many programs and services as part of our commitment to the people and animals of San Francisco:

• An aggressive spay/neuter program has been the cornerstone of The SF/SPCA's work for many years. The Spay/Neuter Clinic, founded in 1978, was the first in the nation to provide low-cost, high-volume spay/neuter surgery.

• In an effort to make the city a community of safe dogs and responsible dog owners, the SF/SPCA has taken the lead in educating the public about dog behavior by offering a variety of public dog training classes.

• The renowned Academy for Dog Trainers offers a comprehensive, progressive education for companion dog professionals.

OUR MISSION

The San Francisco SPCA is dedicated to:
• Saving homeless dogs and cats
• Providing lifesaving care and treatment
• Helping pets stay in loving homes
• Cultivating respect and awareness for the rights and needs of animals
• Affirming the importance of the human-animal bond.

• Our Hearing Dog Program trains former shelter dogs to be assistants and companions for individuals who are deaf or hard-of-hearing,

• The Animal Assisted Therapy Program, which was the first in the nation, brings the healing presence of animals to people in health care facilities citywide.

• Humane Education offers interactive classroom presentations that teach school-children empathy, compassion and respect for life. Summer Camps and Junior Volunteer Programs extend education and service opportunities to many more youngsters, including low income and disadvantaged children.

• Our Foster Care Program network extends lifesaving nurturance, at home, to dogs and cats that are too young, sick or injured to be immediately adopted.

OUR VISION

San Francisco was the first city in the nation to guarantee a home for every adoptable dog and cat. No longer are healthy, well-behaved shelter animals routinely killed to make way for incoming animals. The SF/SPCA's life-affirming vision for the future of animal welfare in San Francisco is now a reality. A practical, policy of low-cost, spaying and neutering of all companion animals, and public education programs, have resulted in record low shelter intake levels. The save rate has soared. San Francisco is now widely recognized as the safest city in the nation in which to be a homeless pet.

• The Feral Cat Assistance program has developed a comprehensive project to trap feral cats, spay or neuter them, and then return them to their habitat, under the supervision of dedicated caregivers.

• The SF/SPCA Sido Program offers an innovative plan for the care of pets, should their owners predecease them.

To learn more about The SF/SPCA, please visit us online at www.sfspca.org

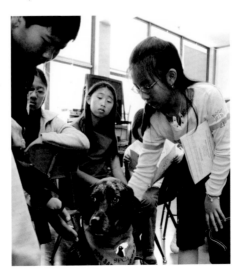

HOW YOU CAN HELP

Volunteer. The SF/SPCA has a team of approximately 900 dedicated volunteers who perform vital, lifesaving services for our shelter animals. Aspiring volunteers attend a basic orientation, and further training is provided for many of the volunteer positions. Call 415-554-3087 to register for an orientation and to join the volunteer team.

Donate. The SF/SPCA is a private, animal welfare organization, supported solely by donations. Contributors help make the world a better place for homeless companion animals.

Friends of San Francisco Animal Care and Control (FSFACC)

We are the only nonprofit raising funds for the city's open-door animal shelter, San Francisco Animal Care and Control (ACC), and its partnering rescue groups, in order to establish or enhance programs of humane welfare, comfort and placement, public services and humane education.

Because ACC must share city revenues with approximately 75 other agencies—and because animals are not as high on the city's list of priorities as those benefitting humans—the city severely limits ACC's budget.

FSFACC has worked to improve this situation. Other city departments have nonprofit Friends-style support organizations. The agency responsible for our city's homeless, abandoned and surrendered animals deserves at least as much. That's why FSFACC is "coming to the rescue."

Accomplishments

- We subsidize free microchipping of the public's dogs and cats, guaranteeing a speedy reunion of lost pets with their families, should the pets get lost. As of June 2005, we microchipped almost 2,000 dogs and cats.

- We fund PetHarbor.com, an online lost pet reunion system for ACC. Anyone can search online for lost pets and look for pets available for adoption. We continue to fund the annual license renewal and service agreement for this sophisticated and valuable program.

- We gave grants to 13 rescue partners that work directly with ACC, saving animals who might otherwise be euthanized due to reversible medical and behavioral problems.

- We have paid for numerous necessities at ACC, including the training of staff at a national conference, volunteer smocks, blankets for the cats, vet "scrubs," kitten formula, and a $20,000 dog group socialization training program, which has resulted in a higher adoption rate and happier dogs during their stay at the shelter.

Goals *(Other services in the works)*

- A small animal adoption campaign, including a public service announcement, classroom activity kits for grade school kids, and information packets for small animal adopters.

- An education program and hotline on how to control and care for the city's homeless cat population.

- Additional grants to ACC's rescue partners. The more money we can channel to them, the more animals' lives we will save.

You can be a rescuer too by becoming a Friend of ACC. Improve the future of the animals in our community. Please join us.

OUR MISSION

To raise funds for ACC and its rescue partners in order to enhance or establish programs and services that benefit animals and serve and educate the public.

OUR VISION

To help ACC and its rescue partners find loving families for every adoptable pet and make the last days or hours of life of a terminally ill or injured animal as pain-free and comfortable as possible. We believe that with sufficient funding ACC can become a leader in the no-kill movement and a model animal shelter for our nation, and the world.

OUR ORGANIZATION

We have no paid officers or staff. FSFACC is a completely volunteer organization. We also work out of our homes or at ACC and so have no office rental expenses. Other than funds needed to produce events, flyers or mailings (a lean five percent of revenues), all contributions directly support the animal welfare services of ACC and its rescue partners.

TO DONATE

FSFACC, P.O. Box 2443
San Francisco, CA 94126-2443
or
online via Local Independent Charities:
http://www.lic.org/search/detail.asp?ID=6992

Rocket Dog Rescue
Saving Animals at the Speed of Light!

*"We rescue not for politics, fortune, or fame, my friend…but for the kiss of a dog." -*PALI BOUCHER

Champion of the forgotten, the abused and the lost, Pali Boucher, founder of Rocket Dog Rescue (RDR), has dedicated her life to saving dogs who otherwise had no hope of rescue. Pali, a San Francisco native, knows something about being forgotten: "I grew up with a mom who was on drugs, homeless and had a lot of mental health problems. It was the '60s. They called them communes, but we were really livin' in the bushes. She died when I was 10."

After that, Pali was in a foster home for a short time and then found shelter in abandoned train cars, old warehouses and junkyards. Homeless, and in and out of jail until 1994, Pali credits the boundless love of her hounddog, Leadbelly, with helping her turn her life around. Concerned with caring for Leadbelly properly, Pali entered a drug rehabilitation program. A year later she was clean and sober, in stable housing and attending City College to study art and photography. When Leadbelly died, Pali knew it was time to give canine social outcasts a second chance at life. "Leadbelly was a gift sent to me. Rocket Dog Rescue is really a tribute to him. He helped me learn how to take care of myself by taking care of him."

Since it began in 2001, RDR has saved over 700 dogs. Dogs usually considered unadoptable—toothless, one-eyed, three-legged, geriatric—are the ones Pali feels the greatest affinity and compassion for. "I have a strong connection to them and they to me. They know they are being saved."

RDR is fundraising for their innovative Urban Sanctuary, a vibrant space that will serve as both a home base for RDR and a healing refuge for the community. Plans include a nursery for rescued puppies who would have been euthanized and 24-hour care provided by veterinarian interns. It's also going be a place for people to cuddle with the dogs while enjoying live music, art and movies.

OUR MISSION

Rocket Dog Rescue (RDR) is a 501(c)(3) volunteer-based organization, dedicated to saving homeless and abandoned dogs from animal shelters and situations where they are in danger of abuse, neglect or euthanasia. RDR places non-aggressive dogs into foster homes where they are socialized, spayed/neutered, vaccinated and treated for medical conditions. RDR searches for permanent homes by distributing posters, hosting a website and organizing mobile adoption fairs & special events.

OUR GOALS

Our ultimate goal is to create a world where all companion animals have loving and permanent homes, and where, no good-natured dogs, no matter what their age or condition, are killed in shelters because they are considered surplus or unadoptable.

HOW YOU CAN HELP

Rocket Dog Rescue is run entirely on donations and the efforts of its volunteers. With no salaries or administrative overhead, 100% of every donation goes directly toward saving lives.

TO DONATE

Donations are greatly appreciated and can be made at: *www.rocketdogrescue.org.*
Tel: 415.642.4786.

Volunteers from all backgrounds, including people in recovery programs working to rebuild their lives, will manage the Urban Sanctuary.

Following the phenomenal success of a TV special, Animal Planet is considering RDR for a TV Series. RDR has also been honored with several awards including a 2005 National Points of Light Foundation Award.

Pets Unlimited

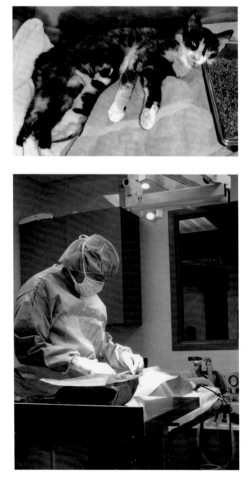

Pets Unlimited was founded in 1947. We are a nonprofit community services organization dedicated to ensuring the humane care and treatment of companion animals. Our vision is for every cat and dog to live a healthy and happy life in a loving home.

We provide high quality, general, specialty, and emergency veterinary medical services. Our hospital operates 24 hours per day, every day of the year. Our veterinarians, technical medical staff, and client services team handle over 40,000 visits per year. We also offer on-site retail services, including pharmacy, veterinary prescription diets, pet products and supplies, grooming, and boarding services.

Our Shelter and Adoption Center (located directly above our hospital) focuses on rescuing and rehabilitating medically and behaviorally challenged animals that have been rejected or scheduled to be euthanized by other shelters or humane societies. Pets Unlimited gives these cats and dogs another chance. In 2004, we adopted out more than 500 animals.

In addition to providing discounted medical services to our own Shelter animals, Pets Unlimited supports other San Francisco animal welfare organizations such as the city's Animal Care and Control, PAWS, Animal Welfare Association, and various rescue groups. We also provide charity medical services to people who are disabled or cannot pay for their service animal's care. The cost totals more than $500,000 per year.

Pets Unlimited is funded in several ways. Our primary financing comes from more than $6 million generated from our veterinary medical services and hospital. Every paying client visit contributes to our organization's mission. The same goes for the proceeds from our pharmacy, retail center, grooming and boarding services. We also receive almost $1 million annually from individuals, organizations, and fundraising events. In addition, more than 300 volunteers provide hundreds of hours in contributed work time.

One of our community outreach activities has been the establishment of an after-school education program. We completed a 12-week pilot program with students from the Marina Middle School in conjunction with the San Francisco YMCA. The program was a hit with the kids, and, thanks to a $10,000 grant from PG&E, it was extended through the 2005 school year.

Support our Shelter by using our Hospital & Veterinary Clinic

Pets Unlimited is a full service veterinary practice supporting not only our shelter animals, but the companion animal needs of the San Francisco and Bay Area community as well. Our veterinary clinic and hospital has a staff of 12 full time doctors and 35 veterinary technicians. We offer 24 hour emergency services, as well as a pharmacy, grooming services, a retail center and special programs such dental and acupuncture services. Our shelter provides a temporary caring home for cats and dogs until they find a permanent loving home. In 2004, Pets Unlimited adopted out over 500 animals! Every client that uses our state-of-the-art veterinary clinic and hospital contributes to the Pets Unlimited mission of providing love and care for our shelter animals until they find their forever home!

OTHER WAYS YOU CAN HELP

Pets Unlimited relies on the support of the people in our community to fulfill its mission of ensuring the humane treatment of companion animals. Because Pets Unlimited focuses on medically and behaviorally challenged animals, some of our 'furry guests' tend to be with us longer than the average shelter animal. Consider sponsoring one or more of our shelter animals during their stay at Pets Unlimited. Your sponsorship will help us provide food, shelter and medical care for our animals until we can place them in a permanent home. We also rely on the generous time commitment our volunteers give us. There are several volunteer opportunities including socializing our animals, visiting convalescent homes and helping at various events throughout the year. We are always in need of foster parents to care for animals until we find them permanent homes. Creating a bequest in your Will or Estate Plan can help ensure we continue our mission. You can also designate a planned gift or join our Furry Friends program. Any donation, large or small makes a difference in the lives of needy animals and is greatly appreciated.

TO DONATE

Pets Unlimited, Attn: Development Dept.
2343 Fillmore Street
San Francisco, CA 94115

Or, via our website:
http://www.petsunlimited.org

Pets Unlimited –
Because Every Life Matters

Ode To My Best Friend

Have you ever licked the face of your best friend? Most people cannot get away with such brazen behavior but you see I'm a Papillion/Pomeranian mix, which gives me some special privileges. You see I am a rescue dog from Hike Animal Rescue. In my 3 years, I have learned that loving is a two way street and I love my new mommy and she loves me! Life was not great before I was adopted but now it is fun!! Sometimes I get to go to rehearsals with my Mommy and watch all of that singing and dancing! Since coming to live with each other, we have had to lean on one another many times. We are very lucky to have found each other. My name is "Happy Go Lucky", but you can call me "Lucky" and now you see why my name fits me so well!!

Tammy Nelson, Steve Silver's Beach Blanket Babylon
Lucky*, Pomerian/Terrier Mix

Amy Tan and Lou DeMattei
Bubba and Lilli, Yorkshire Terriers

Debbie and Des Cussen, Audrey, Chloe
Riley, Welsh Springer Spaniel

Dear riley,
we love You, but I love
You the most of every-
bodyinthe family
love Audrey

Dear Wilbur & Chicita ~

You probably now qualify as the longest "fostered" cats in history. Chicita, you have a sweet and extremely quirky personality ~ you are the only cat I know who can stand on your two hind legs and beg like a dog. You also pick up your food with your paw to eat it ~ yes, you are a very special girl. Wilbur, I knew I was in trouble the first time I saw you in the cage at the shelter ~ one glance at those big black eyes and I was hooked.

My intentions were to foster you _only_ until we found the perfect homes for you, really. Of course, there is no chance of that now, as you are both stuck with us forever. Even though we are expecting our first human baby very soon, I promise you won't become just "the cats". No, you will always be our first babies.

All our Love ~
Mom & Dad

Melinda Bell Conlon and Henry Conlon
Wilbur*, Domestic Long Hair; Chicita*, Tabby Domestic Medium Hair

Mornings on the Hylton Farm start early!

Hannah, William and Babe (Elizabeth) head out to the garage to see all their friends: two guinea pigs, four rabbits, three rats and three mice.

At the sound of the childrens' approach, the two pigs, Avery and Bravery, look at each other and say "here they come, ready ... Pavlov's Dog!" The door opens and they begin their ritual, "squeek, squeeeek, squeeek" ... "they love it when we do that!"

Hannah tells the pigs "we have yummy Butter lettuce leaves for you!" Bravery responds, "gotta cut down on my cholesterol, any carrot tops?!" William reaches for his pig who responds with squeals. "They are squeals of love", William says. "Avery is telling me she loves me!"

"Bravery raises her head high when I pet across her head, she's so brave, that's why I named her Bravery" says Hannah. "I love it when she does that".

The sound of impatient thumps comes from Armand's cage. "Oh, you'll get held too, don't worry". William says to his rabbit, lovingly.

"You know, it is kind of nice having my own cage" says Armand, "but I really liked living with Matilda. Boy, we really had you fooled when the pet store said I was a girl! Amanda and Matilda you named us. But the gig was up when Matilda got pregnant! Now, I'm Armand, Proud Pappa of 6!!!"

Charlotte and Tessa, two beautifully caffed white rats are, by their own admission, the smartest ones on the farm. "We are very well read. When storytime comes each evening, we get to sit on everyones' shoulder and read with the family. We don't even mind sharing space on the bed with that cantankerous, 16 year old cat! His only desire is to rub up against freshly dry-cleaned, black pants!"

"Yes, but that's Mom's cat," say the normally quiet mice. "We're playing it smart, entertaining them with this wheel. Just quiet as church mice, minding our own business so the mrsss will keep a lid on us!

Yup, it's a busy day on the farm! We love it!

Dr. Benjamin and Charlotte Maeck,
Greg and Elizabeth Hylton,
Elizabeth (Babe), William, Hannah
Chester, Tabby Cat;
Katie, Tiger, Bunnies;
Avery, Guinea Pig; Charlotte and
Tessa Van Burgen, Rats

First, I want to thank you again for barking at those guys in front of the liquor store in Oakland who were going to mug me. How'd you know? My ass would have been in a sling!

  - Hey!

Second, the squeak th kitchen door makes will not devour your soul. It's just a door!

  - Hey!

Are you in one of those existential K-holes sometimes, or are you just chilling?

  - [no response]

Hmm. When I squeeze you and talk all goofy, that's because I really love you. Do you know that? Do you know how much I love you?

  - Hey!

Oh yeah, that thing about how you are the greatest dog in the history of canines... that's actually true! Don't let it freak you out.

  - Hey!

Finally, even though mommy and daddy aren't together, we still love you very much. And it was her fault.

  - Hey!

Stephan Jenkins
The Gentle Sweetness Her Goddess is Supreme* (aka The Boo), Pitbull

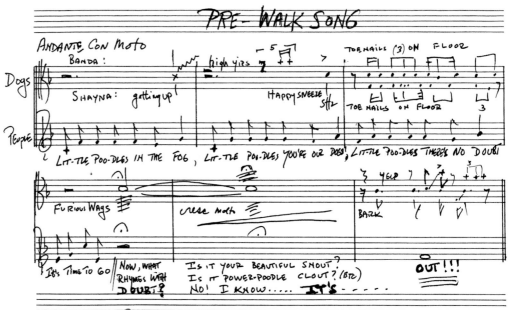

Michael Tilson Thomas and Joshua Robison
Shayna, Standard Poodle;
Banda, Miniature Poodle

Scratch my back!   Feed me!   Need water!

Give me a cookie!   Wanna go out!

Scratch my back more!   GOTTA go out!

Aaaah, ok. Now that you have met my most basic requirements, allow me to share with you, my homo sapien mom, my higher order needs...

Allow me always the freedom to look after you, protect you, warn you. That, after all, is my main goal in life, making sure you are safe (especially from the mailman).

Allow me to play with you, herd you, and run with you. That keeps both of us healthy and happy.

And above all, after 15 years, 2 houses, a husband, 3 kids, and 2 cats (how could you?), allow me just to be with you - at home, in the park, at the beach, in the car. Day or night. Because that's all I really want in this life.

XO XO
Sage

Nancy Sur and Abraham Simmons, Meaza, Campbell, Joseph
Sage, Australian Sheperd; Clover, Cat

I can't do anything about disease
I can't do anything about the hawks
    (nor should I)
But if other human beings should
    threaten your freedom
        or existence

I will do everything I can
    to protect you.
Thousands love you, and I will
call on them to help.

               Mark Bittner

Mark Bittner
Miles, Bukka, Chaplin, and Friends, Cherry-Headed Conures

Jessica McClintock
Coco Chanel, Black Labrador; Lily, Rose, Yellow Labradors

Being a designer of a Romantic Life
Style is exciting but very demanding.
At the day's end -- Home is where
my heart is!
The minute my garage door opens
my three dogs Coco Chanel, Lily and Rose
race to the car for their pats
and hugs -- Coco has such
style and she always comes first
--- then the blond twins Lily and Rose
join in playtime fun -- Being
sisters they are inseparable and
love retrieving balls. These are
my dogs and to me they epitomize
everything that is Romantic about life --
-- Devotion --- Loyalty -- and, of course,
- Unconditional Love --
— Jessica McClintock —

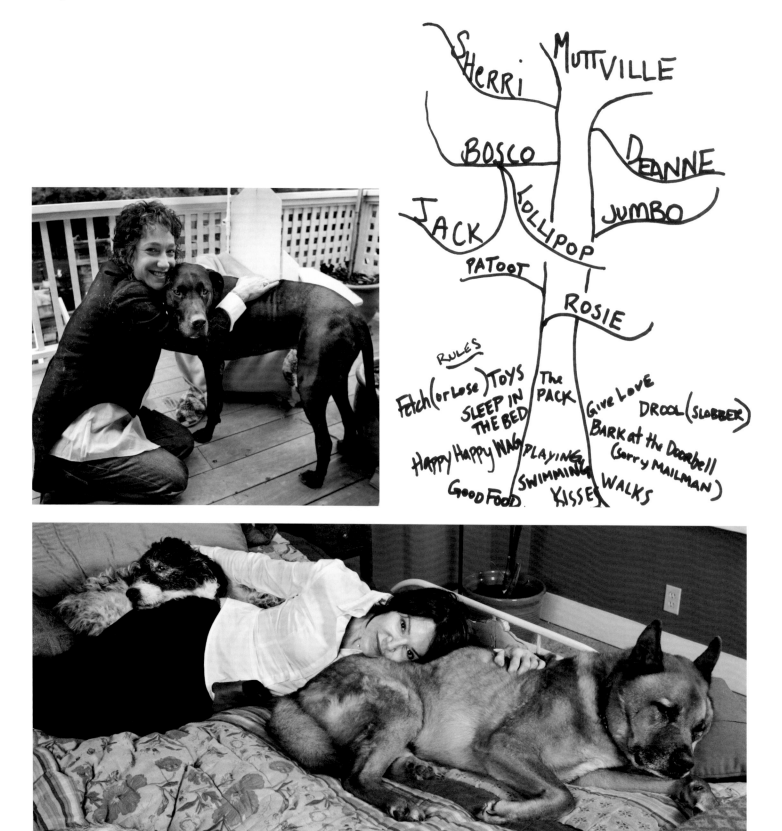

Sherri Franklin and Deanne Franklin
Jumbo*, Pit Bull/Great Dane; Lollipop*, Tasty Mix; Jack the Bear*, Akita/German Shepard; RosieRosebud*, German Shepard Mix

chickens We want our Grubbs - show us your worms.

me Where All The eggs - what do I have to do
To convince you they will never Hatch unless you
brood over them! :

Lynne Foxx
Chickens

A FEW HAIKU

Solitary Viewing
ENTERING THE ROOM
YOU CATCH MY EYE
WHAT ELSE WOULD I LOOK AT
BUT YOU?

Canine Ecstasy
We coo and cuddle
Our non sense
Sounding foolish to anyone
But you.

Is Love Blind?
Entranced by your aquatic world
But wait
How can we eat sushi?

affirmation
treats and toys
from your hands
Would you accept
my gratitude
in kisses?

Richard and Jeanie Schram, Greg
Sterling, Beddington Terrier; Types of Fish: Turquise Discus, Angel, Gold Gourami, Neon Tetra, Clown Loach

Then my mama Ana joined us; she's super nice and I love her soooo much!

I had a sister, her name was Chipi. She was so cool and so loving. She went to live with the angels. I sure do miss her...

Now I have a little brother Arty (he's the little guy in the crazy outfit in the photo). He's really sweet, a truly happy dog! We all have a lot of fun together. We go on lots of walks, get lots of cookies, and kisses galore! Oh, by the way, my name is Cowboy Bunny, but you can call me Bunny...Nice to meet you all!

First there was my mommy Lisa. She's the best mom ever! I was so lucky to get her and she feels lucky to have me too!

GAS

This is my FAMILY!

Lisa Walsh and Ana Olivar
Bunny, Scottish Deerhound; Arty*, Chihuahua/Terrier

My dearest Lola,

I am forever grateful that you came into my life in 1987. You were my canine angel. You taught me patience and kindness and inspired me to become an artist.

And to Nellie, Niblet, Jezebel, Petunia and Caviar each and every morning at the very moment I open my eyes, you are there to shower me with endless kisses and happiness.

You bring joy to my life.
You are my family.

Deborah Grace Kent
Petunia, Caviar, and Niblet, Pomerians; Nellie*, Norwich Terrier; Jezebel, Toy Poddle

Wilkes Bashford
Callie, Long Haired Daschund

CALLIE I hope that I
bring as much happiness
and joy into your life
as you bring into mine.
I LOVE YOU!
Wilkes

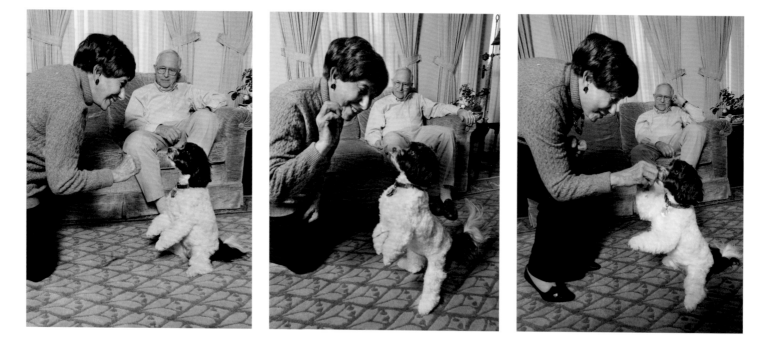

To our dearest Dyna,

It was love at first sight. From the moment we saw you we knew you were going to capture our hearts, and that is exactly what you did.

You spread joy and elicit smiles wherever you go. It is not surprising that you are a successful Animal Assisted Therapy dog. At every Nursing Home or Hospice you visit, you leave the patients feeling happier than they were before you came. There will be a special place in "doggy~ heaven" for you.

You are our best friend and we love you completely.

Dear Mom and Dad,

I am your best girl! I know because you tell me that all of the time. I love you soooo much.

Licks and Wags, Dyna

Loretta and Leonard Levy, Connie
Dyna, Cockapoo

Peter and Stefanie Coyote
Bodhi, Pearl, Mau Cats

To: Peter,
from: Bodhi

I feel so guilty. After all the wonderful food & camaraderie, the petting grooming, and wonderful house and yard, I can't take it any more. I have to confess, when you've been away I've been sleeping with your wife.
        Guiltily,
        Bodhi.

To: Bodhi
from: Peter
    Don't sweat it, guy. I've been sleeping with your sister, Pearl. Man, can she purr!

Patty- Don't you get bored in your cage?

Blue- Naw, I like to chill. Plus I have
    adventures running around the apartment.

P- So can we get a dog or what?

Blue- Only if it lets me ride around
    on its back.

Lindsey- What's your favorite part about
    living here?

Blue- A shoulder-high view of my kingdom.

L- Are you happy?

Blue- Yeah, this is the life...fresh organic
    greens delivered daily, all chopped up;
    I don't have to work for it at all.
    Plus, humans are so amusing.

P/L- If you could change anything,
    what would it be?

Blue- More shoulder-time & to not have
    to share the place with those other
    dragons.

Patty Whalen and Lindsey Miller
Blue, Bearded Dragon

My Dearest Neepie,
Thank you! You have a
wonderful, brave spirit -
you're "wacky!" And your
keen sense of musical -
appreciation is an inspiration
to everyone you meet.
You know, it's always more fun
when you help me put on
my make-up & get ready for
a show!
You're a strange, magical
creature - & always in my
heart.   I love you so.
                  - Ann

Miss Connie Champagne
Professor Neepie*, Persian

Jan and Russ Wahl
Satchmo, Tibetan Terrier

Being with you, Satchmo, is a constant joy. We can never thank you enough for reminding us of what's really important in this life: staying in the Now; appreciating simple things like a snack and a nap; and unconditional love. We named you after our favorite musician Louie Armstrong (his nickname was Satchmo) and on a daily basis you make our hearts sing. Yes.. you are obsessive and __Way__ too smart.. but its all part of the vitality and fun that is you. Thank you for making us better humans. We can only pray that other dogs are as loved as you are and as well cared for. Its' the least we can do.. and we know you agree! ♡ MOMMY & DADDY

To our Furry Friends, Leeloo & Corbin:

We never imagined the simple joys of having you would bring to our lives.

Thank you Leeloo, for sleeping on our desks under the warmth of the lamp.

Thank you Corbin, for greeting us with wet, sloppy kisses.

Thank you Leeloo, for falling asleep in our arms and purring like a motor.

Thank you Corbin, for making us remember what being children is like.

Thank you both for giving us the warmest welcome every time we walk through the door.

Thank you both for loving us unconditionally, no matter what we look like, how we feel or what we do.

Thank you for making our house a home.

We love you both so much!

Bill →   →Natalia

Natalia Martinez and Bill Parsons
Leeloo*, American Tortoiseshell Cat; Corbin, Black Labrador

DONALD: YOU KNOW, CHIP, PEOPLE START TO LOOK LIKE THEIR DOGS AFTER A FEW YEARS. DO YOU THINK SUGAR RAY LOOKS LIKE US?

Chip: If he looked like the two of us, he'd be a Dalmatian.

DONALD: WELL, EVEN IF WE DON'T LOOK LIKE HIM, I THINK THERE ARE TIMES WHEN IT FEELS LIKE SUGAR RAY IS OUR "LOVE CHILD"...

Chip: Yes, I often think he's inherited certain qualities from you & others from me.

DONALD: HE EATS HIS MEALS IN NO TIME FLAT... JUST LIKE YOU!

Chip: He's a lean muscle machine... not an ounce of fat— I don't think he got that from me.

DONALD: JUST LIKE YOU, SUGAR RAY IS SO LOVABLE. AND, ALSO LIKE YOU, HE WEARS HIS HEART ON HIS SLEEVE... ONLY IN HIS CASE, IT'S A SOUL PATCH ON HIS CHEST.

Chip: He's incredibly energetic and has the stamina of the Energizer Bunny &, just like you, he can fall asleep the moment he puts his head on his pillow.

DONALD: HIS FAVORITE SPOT AT HOME IS THE SAME AS YOURS.

Chip: His Kennel?

DONALD: NO, SILLY, THE SUN-DRENCHED OUTDOOR DAY BED WITH THE DOWNTOWN VIEW.

Chip: I only wish we got the attention from strangers that he gets when we walk down the street.

DONALD: SUCH STYLE, LOOKS & GRACE... HARD TO BELIEVE HE'S FROM FRESNO!

Donald Graves and Chip Conley
Sugar Ray, Viszla

Suzzi,
   I really enjoyed our photo shoot at SBC Park. Your mommy tells me that you are a frequent visitor and you love running on the field. Maybe someday my dogs Chucky and Alfie can join you. I love animals and they love me in return. I think that if you don't like animals, you have no heart.

Love,

Orlando Cepeda

Orlando Cepeda
Suzzi*, Shitzu

Simone Neuraumont, Jacob
Captain Jack Sparrow*, Persian

In the last room we found Captain Jack Sparrow. Of all the cats in that shelter the old Captain was the only one who showed any interest in my son Jacob. He went right up to Jacob and rubbed up on his little leg. Each cat had a one page description posted on the door of their cell. Jack Sparrow had a rap sheet a mile long, as his shredded ear and missing eye attested to. And yet here he was cuddling up to my small son, docile as you please. "I choose you" said the Captain. Old Jack Sparrow wasn't long for this world. He's got a new lease on life. Captain of our small two bedroom ship.

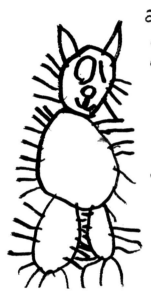

O Romeo, Romeo.

Where for art thou Romeo?

I know where thou art – thou art in my heart!

The Cable car couldst take thee far....

Ah but to ride the BART with thee from the end to the start.....there's the rub.

And so, my dear pet.....whither thou goest, I must go.....to pick up what thou doest, for the law says it is so.

And what of the beloved Juliet, Bella, Bissel, Pilar, Madison, Beatrice, and Carly?

No matter. Sweet Romeo, thou art my love for now and all time!

Love, Mommy

Lisa Uroman
Romeo*, Australian Cattledog Mix

Jean and Bill Coblentz
Arthur*, Mixed Terrier; Chewy*, Tibetan Terrier

Dear Arthur & Chewy -
We love you both.
Chewy - You are a cute adorable 25 pound lap dog.
You crave attention with your jumping into the
lap of anyone who is sitting down and with your
serenade of various squeaks and little woofs.
Arthur - Yes, at times you are difficult to be with, but
we have never regretted your being part of our
family. Stay as sweet as you are.
                    love
                    Mommy and Daddy

Dear Mommy and Daddy -
It's me, Arthur. Thank you for rescuing me.
My disposition is not the best. I get along better
with humans than my own species, yet I know you
care. I am so grateful to share your home and
walking and companionship with you. Just keep
scratching my tummy.

You rescued me too and I love the name Chewy.
My new identity makes me feel reborn. I was
rescued by the SPCA from the Stockton pound and
I never got any attention so I now love being
with you.
                    love,
                    Arthur and Chewy

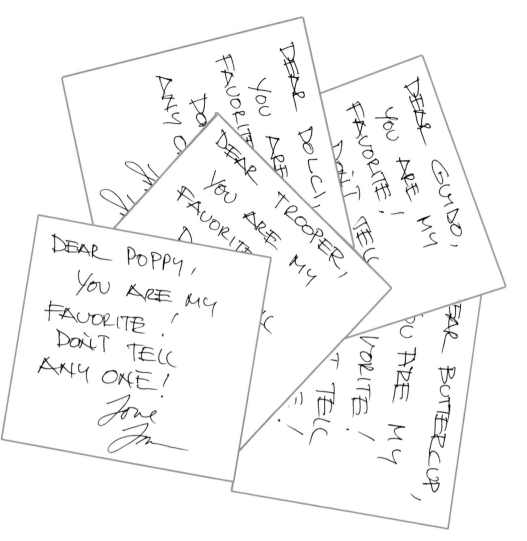

DEAR POPPY,
YOU ARE MY
FAVORITE!
DON'T TELL
ANY ONE!
Love
[signature]

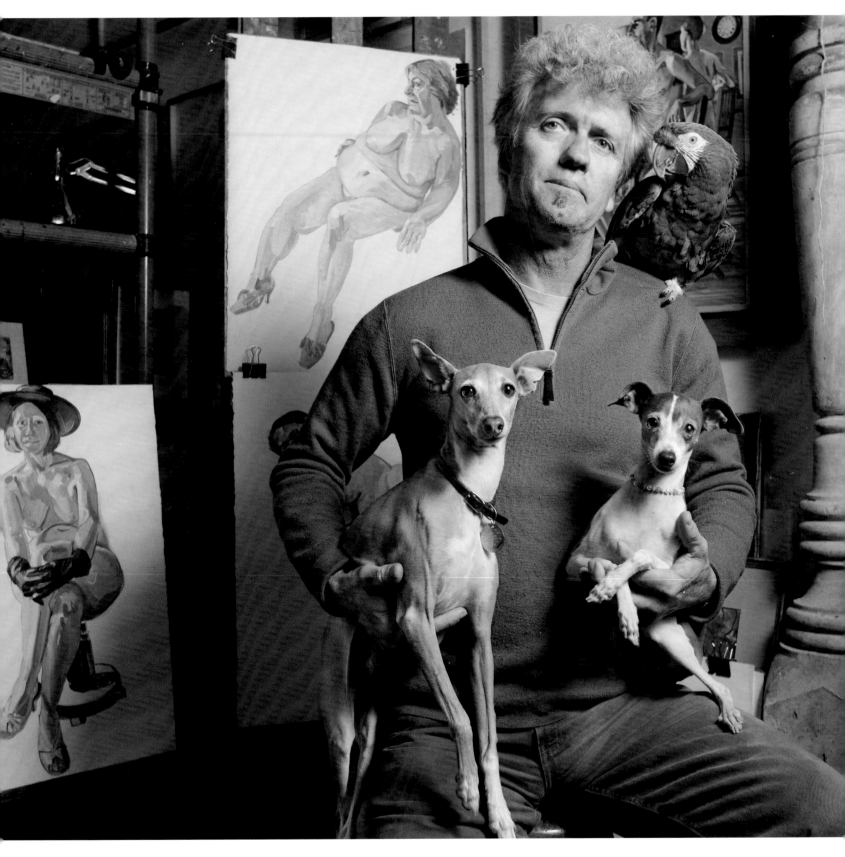

Tom Mogensen
Poppy*, Macaw; Guido* and Dolci*, Italian Greyhounds

Right now we have a 16 year old, a 15 year old, a 14 year old and a 1 year old. The 15 year old and the 1 year old have paws.

Domino - You are the salt of the earth. Sweet, intuitive and intelligent, you have been there throughout the preschool years, the middle school years and even now, the high school years. My faithful carpool companion. My trusty grocery store passenger. We used to run together in the day for pleasure and exercise - and in the night to calm a fearful child in a dark bedroom. Now, you sit by my feet as I return emails and you hear only the very loudest noises. We have raised a family together. You are Revered. You are loved. How I wish you would be here to soften the empty nest.

Snicker Doodle - You are the future. Your fuzzy face, your befuddled expression, your happy-go-luckiness. You lack discretion, you lack manners. You are our sweet, tow-headed toddler. You steal stuffed animals and even lingerie from unsuspecting teenagers. They chase after you. You place sloppy kisses on Domino's face. She tolerates your youthful antics. She knows you are the future.

But for the present, we are all 6 here - sharing our full nest. It's the best.

Jim and Bethany Hornthal, Josh, Becca
Domino*, Border Collie Lab Mix; Snicker, Goldendoodle

Dear Mommy and Daddy,

I am trying to be a good role model for my brother Boomer but it's not going so well. He calls me a kiss-ass just because I am so social with all your friends. I just don't know why he is so reluctant to spread doggie kisses around!! I love it!!

I thank the big doggie in the sky every day that you love me the way you do and that we are a family. xxx ooo love

Andy

Dear Mom and Dad,

So, why I am not like that suck-up Andy? — for starters, he has 3 names — I have at least 10: Boomer, Booey Looey, Boomy, Booboo, Baby Booey, Loo loo, Boobalaloobala (how did you come up with that??), Booiehead, Boomie Toomie, Boobaloo...

Do you have any idea what I go through? I am exhausted trying to figure it out so I have to hide to get some rest.

Yeah, I guess I like the hugging, petting & kissing — after all — I am a cutie-patootie (yet another name, FYI).

Boomer

Emily Scott Pottruck and David Pottruck
Andy, Boomer, Yorkshire Terriers

Your Photo or Note

Your Photo or Note

Pet Cemetery at the Presidio of San Francisco

Pet Cemetery at the Presidio of San Francisco

Gratitudes and Acknowledgements

"Diving into the deep end of the pool without checking to see if there is water" is how a friend once described my actions. Thankfully, I have many lifeguards ready, willing and able to keep me afloat. I could fill pages with "thank-you" to all who contributed in some way to *Tails of Devotion*, particularly:

Thank you to Dr. Douglas Bryant and the staff at Avon Pet Centre, Dr. David Matthiesen and the staff at Animal Hospital Center in Highlands Ranch, Dr. Marguerite Knipe and the students and staff at UC Davis, Dr. Joseph Lynch, and the staff at Pets Unlimited for saving Andy's life and mine as well. Andy has brought more joy to more people than you can ever imagine.

To the godmother of Andy and Boomer, my mentor, guide, boggle competitor, tour de force, neighbor, and partner in doggydom, Amy Tan. "Thank you" does not begin to describe my gratitude for all that you do. I have had the good fortune to experience your magical and marvelous ways and I am a far better person because of you.

I am beyond fortunate to have friends who are supportive and willing to share their perspectives and contacts; thank you for everything and then some to Sarah Cooper, Chris Barnett, Nancy Sur, Karen Cashen, Sherri Franklin, Lis Petkevich, and Carmen Baez.

Leslie Waltzer's work portrays her spirit and her talent; both of which are exquisite. From spending hours of shooting photos to capture the images of devotion to hours in the car and telephone to hours on the computer; Lacy Atkins, you have made an indelible mark on my world. I am grateful to Jocelyn Knight for jumping in at a crucial time and using her expert eye behind the camera to continue our project. Women rule!

Thank you, Heidi Emmel-Anders. Sitting across from me and listening to me go on and on…and on for all these months should have earned you hazard pay. Our dear Marcelina Oliquino, we are blessed to have you in our lives. Thank you for maintaining our sanity and being a great #2 Mom to Andy and Boomer.

To Linda Stoick, Jim Krieg, Kathi Kamen Goldmark, Henry Pilger – thank you for your professional guidance. Thank you, Kristen Green, for your marketing and promotional prowess. David Weinfeld created our website – thank you for your knowledge and flexibility. Thank you, Bryan Bailey, for your masterful finishing touches.

My efforts pale in comparison to all those angels I have met at The SF SPCA, Pets Unlimited, PAWS, Rocket Dog Rescue, Friends of San Francisco Animal Care and Control. I especially thank Bill Hamilton, John Lipp, Pali Boucher, Tina High, Melinda Bell and Joe O'Hehir. To you and your colleagues, I am forever humbled by your devotion and selflessness.

Dearest David. How many times did you hear me say, "I want to write a book." And how many times did you say, "Go ahead." You have opened my world to include more than I ever thought possible. Thank you for loving me and learning to love all my idiosyncrasies (what idiosyncrasies?!?!) and for building a life together. Finally, my parents (all three of them) taught me to be grateful for what I have and to give back; I thank you for that most important life lesson.

Resources

PAWS
645 Harrison Street, Suite #100
San Francisco, CA 94107
www.pawssf.org
Tel: 415.979.9550
E-mail: info@pawssf.org

The San Francisco SPCA
2500, 16th Street
San Francisco, CA 94103
www.sfspca.org
Tel: 415.554.3087

The Friends of San Francisco Animal Care and Control (FSFACC)
P.O. Box 2443
San Francisco, CA 94126-2443
www.fsfacc.org
Tel: 415.822.5566
E-mail: helpanimals@fsfacc.org

Rocket Dog Rescue
P.O. Box 460826
San Francisco, CA 94146
www.rocketdogrescue.org.
Tel: 415.642.4786
E-mail: info@rocketdogrescue.org

Pets Unlimited
2343 Fillmore Street
San Francisco, CA 94115
www.petsunlimited.org
Tel: 415.775.2573
E-mail: donations@petsunlimited.org

Photography

Lacy Atkins
lacyatkins.com
lacyatkinsphotography@comcast.net

photo credits: cover photos, iv, vi, viii, ix, x, 2-19, 24-27, 30-33, 36-49, 52-55, 68-75, 80-81, 84-99, 102-105, 108-109, 114-115, 120-121, 124, 128-129

Jocelyn Knight
JocelynKnight.com
P.O. Box 499
Corte Madera, Ca 94976
phone 415.927.1505

photo credits: xii, 1, 20-23, 28-29, 34-35, 50-51, 66-67, 76-79, 82-83, 100-101, 106-107, 110-113, 116-119, 122-123,125

Graphic Design
Leslie Waltzer
CrowfootDesign.com
leslie@crowfootdesign.com
phone 510.893.3647

Internet & Email Marketing
David Weinfeld
david@zdmgroup.com
phone 415.602.2547

Publicity & Event Planning
Kristen Green
www.kristengreen.com
kgreenpr@kristengreen.com
phone 415.567.2999; 516.983.5511

Digital Imaging/Photo Retouching
Bryan Bailey
Restoration, Photoshop Training
bbailey@alamedanet.net
phone 510.337.9004

Sophie, Miniature Schnauzer and Chupee, Yorkshire Terrier
Pottruck Granddogs - the "next" generation